CONVERSATION WHAT-TO-SAY-AND-HOW-TO-SAY-IT

Being an Efficient Speaker - Do You Have What it Takes?

BY

JACOB GREY, 2022

TABLE OF CONTENTS

Conclusion

Conversation is reciprocal—Good conversationalists cannot talk to the best advantage without confederates. As in whilst it is the combination

Society—The Elements of Good Conversation—What It Is Not—Genius and Scholarship Not Essential to Good Conversation.

CHAPTER ONE

WHAT CONVERSATION IS AND WHAT IT IS NOT

Good conversation is more simply described by what it is not than by what it is. To reach any conclusions on this issue, one needs first determine: What is the objective of conversation? Should the objective be to make interaction with our fellows a free school in which to gain information; should it be to distribute knowledge; or should the purpose be to divert and to amuse? It could appear that any person with a good topic must communicate well and be fascinating. Alas! highly developed individuals are frequently the most quiet. Or, if they speak well, they are likely to talk too well to be excellent conversationalists, as did Coleridge and Macaulay, who spoke long and hard about intriguing things, but were still noted as bores in conversation because they talked at people instead of conversing with them. In society Browning was pleasant in his conversation. He would not debate poetry, and was as chatty on the topic of a sandwich or the exploits of some woman's train at the last drawing-room as on more substantial issues. Though to some he may have looked esoteric in his skill, everyone agreed that he was plain and natural in his talk. Whatever he spoke about, there could not be a moment's question as to his meaning.

From these facts about three men of brilliance, it may be drawn that we do not go into society to acquire education for free; that excellent conversation is not always a vehicle of knowledge; that to be natural, easy, joyous, is the catechism of good chat. No matter how smart a man is, he is frequently cast among common humans; and the ordinary mortals have as much right to discuss as the amazing ones. One may envisage, on the other hand, that when geniuses have opportunity to interact in society their aim is to escape from the concerns which everyday load their brains. If they wish to restrict themselves to an exchange of ideas aside from their unique task, they have a right to do so. In this withdrawal of persons of brilliance from addressing the very things with respect to which their judgment is most useful, there is no question of a significant loss to the world. But until they voluntarily bring out the matter of their work, it must stay in abeyance. Society has no right to coerce their addressing it. This brings us, therefore, to the conclusion that the objective of conversation is to divert, to interest, to entertain; neither to teach nor to be taught, except incidentally. In excellent conversation individuals contribute their charm, their gaiety, their humor, certainly—and their knowledge, if they will. But discourse which essentially entertains is not essentially rubbish. Someone has made this subtle distinction: "I enter a place full with lovely people as I go to view a painting, or listen to a song, or as I dance—that I may amuse myself, and invigorate myself, and elevate my natural spirits, and laugh dull concern away.

True, there must be thoughts, as in all amusements worthy of the term there is a certain seriousness difficult to explain; only they must be kept in the background."

The objective and intent of dialogue is, therefore, pleasure. This agreed, we can establish its constituents. Conversation, above all, is dialog, not monologue. It is a collaboration, not an individual issue. It is listening as well as talking. Monopolizing rulers of society who would allow no dog to bark in their presence are not conversationalists; they are lecturers. There are lots of persons who, as Mr. Benson says, "possess every qualification for chatting except the capacity to communicate." There are many folks who give one monolog after another and call their discourse discussion. The excellent conversationalists are not the ones who dominate the discourse at every meeting. They are the folks who have the grace to offer something of their own while graciously pulling out the best that is in others. They venture themes for debate and attempt each to provide to the other the possibility of building upon them.

Conversation is the exchange of ideas; it is the readiness to transmit thinking on all matters, personal and global, and in turn to listen to the thoughts of others about the ideas offered.

Good conversation is the nimbleness of mind to grasp the chance phrase or the inadvertent topic and play with it, and make it pass from guest to visitor at dinner or in the drawing-room. It is the discussion of any issue whatsoever, from religion to the fashions, and the avoidance of any feature of any subject which would drive the irascible talker to disagreement. As expressed by Cowper in his essay, "Conversation":" Ye powers who command the tongue, if such there be, And make colloquial bliss your care, Preserve me from the thing I fear and hate a fight in the shape of an argument." Wearing one's heart on one's sleeve is excellent for one conversationally. Ready converters are persons who provide their thinking to others in abundance; who make others feel a familiar pulse. No one can reach so close to us as the true talker, with his compassion and his ready comments.

Luther, who stands out as one of the titans of the Renaissance, came into intimate personal contact with his companions in chat; in conversation with him they could always sense his furious and steady pulse.

Another essential of effective discussion is good-humored tolerance, the ability to suffer rubs unavoidably occasioned. The talker who cavils at everything that is uttered interrupts discussion more than if he responded simply yes or no to all things addressed to him. Still another part of successful conversation is the proper type of gossip; gossip which is present and past history of people we know and of people we don't know; gossip which is in no way a temptation to distract.

Raillery may also become a respectable aspect of excellent discussion, if the mockery is like a decent parody of good literature in no way malevolent or ordinary. "Shop," if beautifully matched to the conversational situations, may have its fair place in engaging chat. Friends frequently gather together only to talk things over, to acquire each other's point of view, to hear each other relate of his own concerns, of his job and of his development.

"Shop" chat was sometimes the core of those renowned talks of the seventeenth century coffee-house. Anecdotes are a natural component of communication, yet they become the plague of chat unless maintained under tight constraint. There are times when effective conversation involves brief quiet rather than speaking. It is only the haranguers who consider it their duty to break in with meaningless and disingenuous speech upon a nice and natural moment. An aspect of the good fellowship of permissible discussion is what one would term "interest inquiries." "Interest queries" are simply what the words suggest, and have about them no hint of the nosy and impertinent catechizing which only idiots, and not even knaves, engage in.

The negative phase of dialogue may mostly emerge out of a discussion of the good. By finding what communication is, we uncover, in a measure, what it is not. It is not monolog nor monopolizing; it is not lecturing nor haranguing; it is not detracting gossip; it is not ill-timed "shop" chat; it is not disagreement or discussion; it is not stringing tales together; it is not inquisitive nor impertinent asking. There are yet additional things which discussion is not: It is not cross-examining nor bullying; it is not over-emphatic, nor is it excessively forceful, not persistently controlling, discourse. Nor is excellent conversation grumbling babble. No one can play to advantage the conversational game of throw and catch with a partner who is always pelting him with complaints. It is out of the question to expect anyone, whether stranger or familiar, to choke in pleasant sympathy with minor troubles. The trifling and twisted annoyances of one's own existence are suitable themes for discourse only when they lead to a discussion of the phase of character or the fling of destiny on which such-and-such happenings shine light, since the flow of the thinking then invites a tossing back of ideas.

Perhaps the most crucial thing which excellent communication is not, is this: It is not talking for effect, or hedging. There are two sorts of hedging in conversation: one which results from failing to follow the course of the debate; another which is the consequence of talking at random solely to create bulk. The first is passable;

the last is contemptible. The instant one starts to speak for effect, or to hedge flippantly, he is talking insincerely.

And when a good converser runs against this type of talker, his heart screams out, like Carlyle, for an empty room, his tobacco, and his pipe. It is stated by some one that there are three sorts of a bore: the one who describes the plot of a play, the one who narrates the tale of a book, and the one who tells his dreams. This may be going too far with respect to dreams; because dreams, if handled in the correct manner, are easily made a part of intriguing discussion. But in advanced culture novels and plays are discussed primarily by talking about the prevalent notion around which the plot centered. They are critiqued, not outlined. The most knowledgeable and polished talkers do not attempt the arduous and unrewarded accomplishment of presenting a succinct overview of storylines.

Good conversation, then, is the give and take of talk. A person who converses well also listens well. The one is inseparable from the other. Anything can be talked about in cultivated society provided the subjects are handled with humanity and discrimination. Even the weather and the three dreadful D's of conversation, Dress, Disease, and Domestics, may be made an acceptable part of talk if suited to the time, the place, and the situation. Nor is genius or scholarship essential to good conversation. The qualities most needed are tact, a sincere desire to please, and an appreciation of the truth that the man who never says a foolish thing in conversation will never say a wise one.

CHAPTER TWO

DISCUSSION VERSUS CONTROVERSY

Dr. Johnson's and Robert Louis Stevenson's Opinion of Discussion—Politeness and Discussion—The Hostess in Discussion—Flat Contradiction in Discussion—Polemical Squabbles—Brilliant Discussion in France—The Secret of Delightful

Conversation in France—Leading the Talk—Topics for Discussion—Gladstone's Conversation.

CHAPTER TWO

DISCUSSION VERSUS CONTROVERSY

Many individuals dislike to debate, but these are generally those on the halfway level of the conversational ladder; those to whom the thrill of the amiable intellectual struggle is unknown, and to whom the greatest standards of the art of talking do not appeal. Where there is substantial intellectual activity debate is going to emerge, for the simple fact that individuals will not think alike. Polite debate is the most difficult and the most delightful goal of society as it is of literature; and why should vocal discussion be less appealing than written? Dr. Johnson used to express unbounded hatred for any conversation that was not debate; and Robert Louis Stevenson has told us plainly his view: "There is a particular attitude, aggressive at once and respectful, ready to battle yet most reluctant to quarrel, which stamps out at once the talkable man. It is not eloquence, nor justice, nor obstinacy, but a specific amount of all these that I prefer to meet in my amiable opponents. They must not be pontiffs maintaining dogma, but huntsmen questing seeking components of truth.

Neither must they be boys to be trained, but fellow-students with whom I may dispute on equal terms." From Mr. John B. Yeats, one of the numerous Irishmen who have written tellingly on this important topic of human connection, we get:

"Conversation is an art, as literature is, as painting is, as poetry is, and subject to the same rules from which nothing human is barred, not even argument. There is literature which argues, and art which argues, and poetry which argues, so why not dialogue which argues? Only argument is the most difficult to sculpt into the most glorious form of art."

Some individuals envision a perpetual antagonism between civility and sincere debate. Politeness consists, they imagine, in continually replying, "yeah, yes," or at worst a non-committal "indeed?" to every syllable addressed to them. This is likely to be our American voice of conversation, where, for lack of boldness in taking up an issue, communication typically collapses into a succession of tales. In Germany the tendency is to get carried away in conversation to the point of a verbal argument. There is no bigger bore in society than the guy who agrees with everyone. Discussion is the arena in which we evaluate the power of one another's brains and run a friendly tilt in attractive self-assertiveness; it is the common meeting-ground where it is recognized that Barnabas will accept mild reproof from Paul, and Paul take gentle reproof from Barnabas. Those who look upon any disagreement from their opinions as a personal assault to be greeted with signals of hostility are no more suitable for clever conversation than they are fit for life and its vagaries. "Whoso keepeth his lips and his tongue keepeth his soul in peace," it is true; but he also maintains himself dead to all human connection and as colorless in the world as an oyster. "Too strong a desire to please," argues Stevenson, "banishes from discussion anything that is sterling.... It is better to unleash a scream in the form of a theory than to be totally insensible to the jars and incongruities of life and accept everything as it comes in a desolate ignorance." This is equivalent to telling the individual who treads too nicely and fears a shock that he had pleased us better had he pleased us less, which is the subtle observation of Mr. Price Collier writing in the North American Review: "It is perhaps more often true of women than of men that they conceive affability as a concession. At any rate, it is not unusual to find a hostess busying herself with attempts to agree with all that is said, with the idea that she is thereby doing homage to the effeminate categorical imperative of etiquette, when in reality nothing becomes more quickly tiresome than incessant affirmatives, no matter how pleasantly they are modulated. Nor can one escape one of two conclusions when one's conversation is so recklessly consented to: either the speaker is restricting herself exclusively to uncontradictable platitudes, or the listener has no thought of her own; and in either case quiet were golden. In this regard it was good to recollect the very great epigram of the Abbé de Saint-Réal, that 'On s'ennuie presque toujours avec ceux qui l'on s'ennuie.' For not even a lover can fail to be bored at last by the incessant lassitude of agreement manifesting itself in twin feelings to his own. 'Coquetting with an echo,' Carlyle termed it. For, while it may make a man feel intellectually powerful at first, it makes him feel mentally maudlin at last; for, as the Abbé says, to be bored one's self is a definite indicator that one's partner is likewise tired."

Though courteous disagreement is acceptable in dialogue, bald contradiction is despicable. Dean Swift believes that a person inclined to contradiction is better appropriate for Bedlam than for dialogue. In debate, even more than in lighter discourse, decency as well as honor mandates that each party to the conversational game comply with the graces and fairness of it. "I don't think so," "It isn't so," "I don't agree with you at all," are too flat and positive for true delicacy and refinement in conversation. "I had been tempted to believe differently," "I shall be happy to hear your reasoning," "Aren't you mistaken?" are more appropriate expressions with which to begin disagreement. In French culture a disparity of opinions is usually conveyed by some courtesy-phrase, such as "Mais, ne pensez-vous pas" or "Je vous demande pardon"—the urbane alternatives for "No, you are incorrect," "No, it isn't."

Our own Benjamin Franklin, whose appreciation of the conversational art in France won completely the hearts of the French people, tells us in his autobiography that in later life he found it necessary to throw off habits acquired in youth: "I continued this positive method for some years, but gradually left it, retaining only the habit of expressing myself in terms of modest diffidence: never using when I advanced anything that might possibly be disputed, the words 'certainly,' 'undoubtedly,' or any others that give the air of positiveness to an opinion, but rather say, 'it appears to me,' or 'I should think it so-and-so, for such-and-such a reason,' or 'I imagine it to be so,' or it is so 'if I am not mistaken.'" Unyielding obstinacy in dialogue is deadening to communication, and yet the extreme opposite is paralyzing. Open disdain of any effort at warmth of conversation is paralysis and torpor to discourse. When one encounters a hostess, or a conversational partner, "whose sole delight is to be dissatisfied," one is reminded of the railway superintendent who kept the lines hot with fault-finding messages with his initials "H. F. C." until he came to be known along the track as "Hell For Certain." People of a resentful frame of mind, whose every statement is a gamble, and who transform every word into a missile, are appropriate for polemical squabbles, but not for polite debate. Those boisterous folks who, when their opponents seek to speak, shout out against it as a great injustice, are extremely well fitted to connection with Kilkenny cats, but not with human beings. It is in order to conquer by these methods one who could otherwise outmatch them fully that they aim to reduce their opponent to a mere interjection. "A man of culture," adds Mr. Robert Waters, "is not intolerant of disagreement. He freely shares his opinions on any given issue, without hesitating to declare wherein he is uneducated or dubious, and he is ready for correction and illumination wherever he finds it." Such a man never presses his hearers to accept his views; he not only tolerates but considers opposed opinions and listens attentively and respectfully to them. Hazlitt said of the charming discussion of Northcote, the painter: "He lends an ear to an observation as if you had brought him a piece of news, and enters into it with as much avidity and earnestness as if it interested only himself personally."

Of all the tenets of good conversation to which the French give heed, their devotion to listening is the most notable. From this judiciously attentive attitude arises their uninterrupting shrug of acceptance or displeasure. But listening is merely one of their many established conversational dicta: "The talk of Parisians is neither dissertation nor epigram; they have pleasantry without buffoonery; they combine with talent, with genius, and with reason, maxims and flashes of wit, incisive sarcasm, and rigorous ethics.

They run through all subjects that

each may have something to say; they exhaust no subject for fear of tiring their hearer; they propose their themes casually and they treat them rapidly; each succeeding subject grows naturally out of the preceding one; each talker delivers his opinion and supports it briefly; no one attacks with undue heat the supposition of another, nor defends obstinately his own; they examine in order to enlighten, and stop before the discussion becomes a dispute." Such was Rousseau's description of Parisian discourse; and someone else has stated that the French are the only people in the world who comprehend a salon whether in upholstery or chat. "Every Britisher," remarked Novalis more than a hundred years ago, "is an island"; while Heine once characterized silence as "a discussion with Englishmen." We Americans, however not so guarded in speaking as our English brethren, are less courteous to conversational pleasantries; and both of us are well behind the French in the elegant art of verbal expression. Not only is the spoken English of the learned Irish the most cosmopolitan and finest modulated of any English in the world, but the dialogue of sophisticated Irishmen more accurately approaches the perfection of the French.

It is as enlightening to study the finest models in human contact as to study the best models in literature, or painting, or any other art. One of the characteristic aspects in French conversation is that it is generally maintained broad; and by general I mean incorporating in the chat all the conversational group as opposed to tête-à-tête dialog. Many individuals disagree with the French on this. Addison said that there is no such thing as conversation save between two individuals; and Ralph Waldo Emerson and Walter Savage Landor remarked something of the same type. Shelley was obviously a tête-à-tête talker, as Mr. Benson, the present-day writer, in some of his personal chats, asserts himself to be. But Burke and Browning, the best conversationalists in the history of the Anglo-Saxon race, like all the famous women of the French salon, from Mme. Roland to Mme. de Staël, kept pace with any number of interlocutors on any number of subjects, from the most abstruse science to the lightest jeu d'esprit. Good discourse between two is no doubt a duet of exquisite compassion; yet great communication is more like a fugue in four or eight parts than like a duet. Furthermore, general and tête-à-tête conversation have both their place and occasion. At a dinner-table in France private talks are very soon dispelled by some attentive moderator. Dinner guests who commit themselves to one other alone are not tolerated by the French hostess as by the English and American. Because tête-à-tête conversation is considered good form so generally among English-speaking peoples, I have in other essays adapted my comments on this subject to our customs; but talk which is distributed among several who conform to the courtesies and laws of good conversation is the best kind of talk.

In general conversation everyone deserves to have a voice. It is the extreme humility of some and the arrogance and polemical propensity of others that preclude decent broad dialogue. People have only to begin with three axioms: the first, that everybody is entitled, and often bound, to form his own opinion; second, that everybody is equally entitled to express that opinion; and third, that everybody's opinion is entitled to a hearing and to consideration, not only on the ground of courtesy, but because any opinion honestly and independently formed is worth something and contributes to the discussion. Another fundamental of French communication is that it is maintained personal, in the sense, I mean, that the personality of the speakers suffused it. "The topic being adopted," as Stevenson explains, "each talker plays on himself as on an instrument, confirming and defending himself." This counter-assertion of personality, to all appearances, is battle, yet at bottom is friendly.

A topic which is basically generic and impersonal gets lost in the unintentional confrontations of personalities, since the characteristic which plays the most crucial role is presence of mind, not right thinking. A conversationalist whose argument is totally erroneous may frequently, by exercise of linguistic adroitness, dispose of an objection which is actually fatal. The full swing of the personalities of the speakers in a dialogue is what makes the flint strike fire. It is only from heated minds that the true essence of conversation springs; and it is in talk which glances from one to another of a group, more than in dialog, that this personality is reflected. "It is curious to note," says an editorial in The Spectator, "how much dialog there is in the world, and how little true conversation; how very little, that is, of the genuine attempt to compare the distinct bearing of the same issue on the brains of various persons. It is an uncommon thing in the world to arrive, even among the finest writers, on a good picture of the varied viewpoints held by different brains on the same topic, and the causes of the difference."

Quite as evident a feature in French conversation is the attitude of the conversers to their topic. They never strive to resolve problems as if their choices were the ultimate court of appeal, and as if they must make a frenzied effort to take their side of the subject to triumph. They talk for the fun of arguing; not for the pleasure of vanquishing, nor even of persuading. They talk, just; they do not dispute, nor do they plunge into controversy.

One of the major conversational

pleasures of the French is their facility in guiding conversations.
This develops out of a widespread inclination in France to take efforts in communication and to understand its unspoken behest. The uninformed suspect nothing of the understanding and attention which develops even the innate conversational talent of a Madame de Staël or a Francisque Sarcey.
The initiated realize that the same factors which make the French phenomenal conversationalists make them competent and

attractive hosts and hostesses. The talker who can follow in conversation understands how to lead, and vice versa.

Without a leader or "moderator," as the great Scotch phrase has it, discourse is liable to become either lukewarm or demoralized; and frequently, for the absence of good and sophisticated directing, debate that might otherwise be brilliant deteriorates into chaos. As strange as it may seem at first, it is still true that excellent communication is impossible if there is too much speaking. Some type of order must be silently if not instinctively maintained, else the phrases clash in normal discourse. Leading conversation is the adroit speech which checks the refractory conversationalist and changes imperceptibly the subject when it is sufficiently threshed or grows over-heated; it is guiding the talk without palpable break into fresh fields of thought; it is the tact with which, unperceived, the too slow narration of a guest is hurried by such courteous interpolations as "So you got to the inn, and what then?" or, "Did the marriage take place after all?"; it is the art with which the skilful host or hostess sees that all are drawn into the conversational group; it is the watchfulness that sends the shuttle of talk in all directions instead of allowing it to rebound between a few; it is the interest with which a host or hostess solicits the opinions of guests, and develops whatever their answers may vaguely suggest; it is the care with which an accidentally interrupted speech of a guest is resuscitated; it is the consideration which puts one who arrives late in touch with the subject which was being discussed just before his appearance. It is this concern for conversational cues which gives any host or hostess an almost unbounded power in social intercourse; for he is the best talker who can lead others to talk well. It goes without saying that people who have internalized all the previous characteristics of effective conversation are never disconnected in their speaking. Their immaculate talent of hearing is accountable for their proficiency in following the logical drift of the talk. This may be considered a national characteristic. In good French society there are no sudden changes of ideas in the various utterances. The speech of each speaker arises spontaneously out of what some one of his conversational partners has just been saying, or it is suitably prefaced by an introduction statement linking it with a particular prior speech.

They realize that, once launched, no converser can predict where the give and take of discourse will bring him; but they also know that this does not demand unpleasant and direct changes of topic. The weakness of inattention and of unconscious shunting in conversation is essentially uncommon in excellent society in France.

Is it any surprise that in a nation where conversation is regarded as an art susceptible to development and having certain fixed rules, so many French ladies of modest background, like Sophie Arnould and Julie Lespinasse, have earned their way to recognition by their conversational powers? Is it any surprise that in France polite dialogue is considered the most thrilling and enjoyable activity in the world?

One reason there is so little acceptable conversational debate is the indisposition of individuals in society to say what they believe; their hesitation to convey their complete views on any one issue. It is this aspect of unrestrained utterance or disclosure which makes literature engaging; why therefore keep thinking too carefully from conversation? The propensity of dodging is cowardly as well as unsocial; and nothing so augments discussion as being delightfully straightforward; letting others know where to find you.

The most ridiculous beliefs receive respect if stated intrepidly. Sincere speech is required to excellent communication of any type, and particularly is crucial to debate. One of the silliest of conversational faults is quibbling—talking insincerely, merely for the purpose of employing words, and moving the matter at issue to some extraneous, subordinate

argument on which the choice does not at all depend. It is the intellectually honest individual who shines in dialogue.
Another reason why dialogue is fading is the disdain we have for outstanding issues. We merely mention them, or hint at them; and this cannot lead to very clever conversation. Tho prattle and persiflage have their place in discussion, talkers of the highest class weary of incessantly pushing chit-chat. "What a piece of business; monstrous! I have not read it; impossible to acquire a box at

the opera for another week; how do you like my dress? It was much like yesterday at the Bus stop; how horribly your cravat is knotted! Were you aware that it was lost substantially by the collapse of Thursday? That sweet man's passing threw me a nice fit of tears; do you travel this summer? Is Blank actually a genius? It is unfathomable; they married just two years ago.

" This type of agile language is all very well; just because one enjoys syllabub sometimes is no indication that one is prepared to abandon meat

totally.
Conversational themes may be too frivolous for amusement as well as too serious; yet even significant matters might be treated in a light fashion if required. " Clever individuals are the finest encyclopedias," observed Goethe; and the great premier Gladstone was a delightful man in company, but he never spoke on any but serious matters.
He was famous for his ability to suck people dry without appearing in the least to investigate. "True discourse is not satisfied with thrust and parry, with simple sword-play of any

type, but should put mind to mind and expose the actual lines of agreement and the real lines of divergence. Yet this is the precise type of dialogue which seems to me so very unusual." In order that a big subject shall be a good topic of discussion, it must generate an excitement of belief or skepticism; individuals must have determined views one way or the other. I feel with Stevenson that theology, of all things, is an appropriate topic for conversational debate, and for the reason he gives: that religion is the medium through which all the world examines life, and the dialect in which individuals communicate their judgements. Try to chat for any amount of time with individuals to whom you must not discuss creeds, morality, politics, or any other significant interest in life, and notice how inane and fettered discourse becomes.

The peaceful and yet lively discussion of major issues is the most exciting of all discourse. The thing to be wanted is not the avoidance of debate but the fostering of it according to its unwritten laws and principles.

"The first requirement of any discussion at all," says Professor Mahaffy of Dublin, "is that individuals should have their thoughts so far in sympathy that they are prepared to converse about the same topic, and to hear what each member of the group feels about it. The greater requirement which now comes before us is, that the speaker, aside from the content of the discourse, takes an interest in his hearers as different beings, whose thoughts and emotions he seeks to know Sympathy, however, should not be overwhelming in quality, which makes it demonstrative. We have a wonderful term which depicts the over- empathetic individual, and indicates the judgment of society, when we say that he or she is gushing. To be excessively sympathetic makes conversation, which implies diversity of view, difficult." Those who strive to learn how far dialogue is advanced by sympathy and inhibited by over-sympathy; those who endeavor to identify to what extent healthy debate is degraded by caustic dispute, should not be scared of robust intellectual buffeting. Discussion springs from human nature when it is under the influence of strong feeling, and is as much an ingredient of conversation as the vocalizing of sounds is a part of the effort of expressing thought.

Gossip in Literature—Gossip Comes from Being of One Kindred Under God—Gossip and the Misanthrope—Personal History of People We Know and People We Don't Know—Gossip of Books of Biography—Interest in Others Gives Fellowship and Warmth to Life—Essential Difference Between Slander and Innocent Gossip—The Psychology of the Slanderer—The Apocryphal Slanderer—"Talking Behind Another's Back"—Personal Chat the Current Coin of Conversation.

CHAPTER THREE

GOSSIP

It seems surprising that, in all the vast list of excellent dissertations on every topic under the sun, no English writer should have given a word under the tempting heading of "Gossip." Even

Leigh Hunt, who wrote vivaciously and wonderfully on so many light matters, was not lured by the alluring potential of this subject to which both the educated and the unlearned are ready at all times to lend an eager ear or sight. One typically conceives gossip as something to which one gives just one's ear, and never one's sight; yet what are "Plutarch's Lives" but the appropriate type of gossip? That so many literary men and women have vaguely suspected the alluring tone-color of the word "gossip" is proved by: A Gossip in Romance, Robert

Louis Stevenson; Gossip in a Library, Edmund William Gosse; Gossip of the Caribbees, William R. H. Trowbridge, Jr.; Gossip from Paris During the Second Empire, Anthony North Peet; Gossip in the First Decade of Victoria's Reign, Jane West; Gossip of the Century, Julia Clara Byrne; Gossiping Guide to Wales, Askew Roberts and Edward Woodall; Gossip with Girls and Maidens Betrothed and Free, Blanche St. John Bellairs. Yet no one has ever thought of writing about gossip for its own delightful purpose.

Among every-day terms, possibly the word "gossip" is more to be reckoned with than any other in our language. The youngster who rushes confidently to mother to confess his grievance is a gossip; he is also a historian. Certainly gossip is in its tone intimate and personal; it is the familiar and personal touch which makes Plutarch's Lives attractive. At the base of the term "gossip," argue etymologists, there lurks an honest Saxon meaning, "God's sib"—"of one kindred under God."

It would be only a misanthrope who

would declare that he had no interest in his fellows. He is invariably a selfish person who shuns personality in talk and refuses to know anything about people; who says: "What is it to me whether this person has heard Slezak in Tannhäuser; what do I care whether Mrs. So-and-So has visited the French play; what concern is it of mine if Mr. Millions of eighty marries Miss Beautiful of eighteen; what is it to me whether you have watched the agonies of a furnishing party at Marshall Field's and have observed the bridegroom of tender years victimized by his wife and mother-in-law with their appeals to his excellent taste; of what interest to me are the accounts of the dissolute excesses which interspersed the wild outbreaks of religious fanaticism of Henry the Third of France?" This selfish individual is also incredibly foolish, because nothing so augments discussion as a reasonable interest in other people.

"I shook him vigorously from side to side Until his face was blue. Come, tell me how you live, I begged, And what it is you do."

This approach of Alice's Through the Looking Glass ballad singer for shaking speech out of people, however perhaps too vigorous, is less fatiguing than Sherlock Holmes's inductive procedures. Like Sherlock without his excuse, the kind and generous must admit to a huge interest in the problems of others. Gossip is the dialogue of the play of humanity; and we have a right to introduce any harmless and elegant ways of thawing their tales from the performers, and of unwinding dramatic knots. People with good judgment of persons and things collect the fruit of a calm eye; they perceive in the modest world of private life history as fascinating and problems as vast as those that capture our attention in literature, or in the theater, or in public life. Personal gossip in its intellectual form has a fascination not harmful; and it throws fresh insights on character more frequently pleasant than adverse.

There is no difference between loving this intimate chat and enjoying The Mill on the Floss or works of biography.

Boswell, in his Life of Johnson, and Mrs. Thrale, in her Letters, were persistent gossips about the great man. And what an amazing little tattler was Fanny Burney—Madame d'Arblay! Lord William Lennox, in his Drafts on My Memory, is full with irrepressible and intriguing ephemera, from the anecdote of General Bullard's salad-dressing to vital dramatic history linked with the theater of his day. The Spectator was the quintessence of gossip in an era of gossip and pleasant conversation. We might go a great lot farther back to the gossips of Theocritus, who are as vibrant and life-like as if we had just met them in the park. All biography is a putting together of trifles which in the aggregate make up the captivating life-stories of men and women of previous and current preeminence. It is to the gossips of all periods that we owe much of worth in literary history.

Without the personal interest in the circumstances of others which makes gossip conceivable, there would be no fellowship or warmth in life;

social interaction and discussion would be inhuman and lifeless. Mr. Benson in his article "Conversation" warns us that an impersonal talker is likely to be a boring dog. Mr. Henry van Dyke states that the attribute of talkability does not identify a distinction among objects; that it shows a difference among persons. And Chateaubriand, in his Memoirs d'Outre-tombe, confides to us that he has heard some quite delightful accounts turn irritating and nasty in the lips of ill-disposed verbal historians.

One may engage oneself in the dramatic happenings in the lives of one's friends without venting or vilifying their character. Gossip is capable of a more benign aim than traducing others. It is the malignity which converts gossip into scandal against which moderate conversationalists recoil; the type of thing which Sheridan gibbeted in his classic comedy, The School for Scandal:\s"Give me the papers, (lisp) how daring and free! Last night Lord L. was discovered with Lady D.!.!. . . . . . ." So fierce, so rapid, the monster there's no gagging: Cut scandal's head off, yet the tongue is wagging."

But this is scandal, not gossip, and scandal comes from individuals incapable of anything greater either in thinking or speech. Among individuals who understand the art of conversation, libelous talk is seldom heard; among those who nurture it to perfection, never. It is the first commandment of the slanderer to repeat swiftly all the caustic talk he hears, but to keep strictly to himself any good comments or friendly chatter.

Those who see no line between scandal and gossip should note that gossip may be good-natured and commendatory as well as aggressive and unfavorable.

In the published letters of the late James Russell Lowell is an account of his meeting Professor Mahaffy of Trinity College, Dublin, who is reputed to be one of the most delightful of men. They met at the home of a friend in Birmingham, England, and as Lowell took leave of Mr. Mahaffy he remarked to his host: "Well, that's one of the most lovely people I ever met, and I don't mind if you tell him so!" When Lowell's comment was relayed to Mr. Mahaffy, he screamed, "Poor Lowell! to suppose that he can never have met an Irishman before!" And this was gossip as certainly as the antagonistic prattle about Lord and Lady Byron was gossip. No, yes, defamation and libelous discussion are not required parts of gossip. People who take malevolent delight in utilizing words for harmful goals suffer from a mental condition which does not fit within the scope of discourse.

Regarding the mental defects of

individuals who prefer to wallow in the mud of scandalous news about others, the psychologists have arrived at some fascinating findings. To them it appears that there is an underlying identity between gossip and brilliance. In both, the brain processes function with the same urge to recreate every component of prior experience, since both think by what is known as "total recall." From the concept of one item their brains move to all kinds of faraway connections, sane and ridiculous, sensible and grotesque, significant and irrelevant.

The basic distinction between the gossip mind and the genius mind is the capacity of genius to discern between the worthy and the worthless, the trivial and the significant, the real and the false. The ideas of the gossip, so the psychologists tell us, have connection but not coherence; the thoughts of the genius have coherence and likewise connection and unity. Thus we see that scandal-mongers are at fault in the head more than in the heart; and that it behooves those who do not desire to have themselves considered mentally unfit to make a line between scandal and harmless talk. As I have previously remarked, there is nothing so exciting as the dramatic episodes in the lives of human people. Despite the nature- study enthusiasts who appear to reject humans a place in nature, "the true study of mankind is man" and will eternally be such. But this does not imply that mental weaklings should be permitted to find and speak about just scandalous moments in the past of their contacts. The spiteful scandal-monger who defames someone, or hears him defamed or scandalized, and then goes to him with expanded and greatly colored accounts of what was said about him, is the venom of the snake and should not be accepted in society. A sanitarium for mental delinquents is the only fitting location for such a person.

And let me add that the apocryphal slanderer, the guy who never says but indicates all kinds of spiteful things, is the worst form of scandal-monger. The cultured conversationalist who discusses gossip in its intellectual form does not dabble in indirect hints and insinuations. He expresses what he needs to say intrepidly because he says it discriminatingly. Keen judgment which recognizes the basic difference between scandal and fitting personality in discourse brings gossip to the perfection of an art and the dignity of a science. Undiscriminating individuals, then, would best leave personalities alone and stick to the more generic and less resilient themes of talk. Good gossip is accessible only by brains that are capable of far higher conversation than chatter. Cultivated, well-poised, well-disposed folks should never be scared of enjoying their discussion to a certain amount with gossip, since they indulge it in the correct manner. And provided their personal and familiar talk is listened to by equally cultivated, well-poised, and well-disposed people, their gossip need not necessarily be limited to the mention of only pleasant and complimentary history; no more, indeed, than Plutarch found it necessary to tell of the glory of Demosthenes without mention that there were those who whispered graft and bribery in connection with his name. There are a few very good and very dull people who try to stop all adverse criticism. All raillery strikes them as cruel. They would want to have every parody executed by the common hangman. Even the finest of humor is fundamentally unappealing to them.

They want only vividly colored letters from which

every gentle shade of fault has been eliminated. One cannot argue that they have a true love of human nature, since they do not know what human nature is. They are ready to take up arms with it at every point. Such individuals cannot perceive that mockery, or gossip, may be either benign or malevolent; that history can be either skewed or neutral. With many, refusing to accept unpleasant criticism is a simple attitude, while with others it is cynicism. In acquaintance with the illiterate, every well-bred person is rightly appalled by their joy in detraction and in unpleasant news of all kinds. But the disgusting individuals who seek every excuse to malign, and who prefer to hear only the bad of the world, are so unusual as to be unimportant.

These few villains are gone when one talks about incapacity to discriminate between detraction and hostile criticism. Those who can praise effectively are always adept at criticizing badly. They never take their critique too far, nor give purposefully a sour flavor to it.

There is a sad custom that a person should never say something behind another's back which he would not say before his face. This is all quite well so far as it pertains to poisonous lies repeated purposefully to damage; but how colorless are the individuals who never have critical ideas on anything or anyone; or those who, having them, never voice them!

Criticism and cavil are two completely different things. Absence of criticism is absence of the ability of distinguishing.

This era of science has educated individuals to stare reality directly in the face and learn to discriminate. That person to whom everything is sweet does not know what sweet is. The intelligent world, unlike the naive, is not terrified of "passing comments." There is no question that criticism, whether it comes directly or obliquely, adds a horror to life as soon as one drops below a certain degree of development. The uninformed are afraid by the mere concept of criticism; the cultured are not. Perhaps the explanation for this distinction is that ordinary people have a scathing and utterly uncritical critique to fear. In that culture sensitiveness is not very frequent. They are not dishonorable; they are only tough and can perceive no differences. It is not given to these individuals to laud logically and to condemn discriminatingly. Vilifying statements are said and repeated among them which bright people would be incapable of expressing. The educated not only adopt a softer way of communication, but also avoid repeating things, except with a discriminating intention to be helpful to others. The cultivated who have raised life to a much higher degree than the uncultivated have secured their liberty by a social law.

They say what they like, and it does not come to the ears of the person about whom they have spoken it. And if it did it wouldn't matter much. Criticism which is critically presented is generally critically accepted. The maliciousness of critical criticism rarely rests in the individual who expresses it, but in the person who conveys a narrative. The instant knowledgeable individuals find that one among them has venomously repeated a negatively critical comment, they quickly realize that that person is not of the manner born. There is no surer evidence.

If the born advocate is not necessarily a saint, the born critic is not always a sinner. Robert Louis Stevenson understood the importance of the personal touch in conversation when he wrote: "So far as conversational subjects are truly talkable, more than half of them may be reduced to three: that I am I, that you are you, and that there are other people dimly understood to be not quite the same as either." So, again, did Mr. J. M. Barrie, when he informed us that his beloved Margaret Ogilvy, in spite of little personal interest in Gladstone, "had a strong confidence in him as an aid to discourse. If there were mute males in the gathering, she would give him to them to speak about just as she would split a cake among children."

It is often hinted by men that women are made good conversationalists by a sense of irresponsibility. But I am inclined to think that a little gossip now and then is relished by the best of men as well as women. The tendency to gossip with which men constantly credit women, and in which tendency the men themselves keep pace, helps both men and women very effectively to have a good conversation. "It is more necessary," argues Stevenson again, "that a person should be a good gossip and chat pleasantly and briskly about ordinary people and the thousand and one nothings of the day and hour, than converse with the tongues of men and angels Talk is the creature of the street and market-place, feasting on rumor; and\sits final recourse is still in a dispute about morality. That is the heroic type of gossip; heroic in virtue of its lofty pretensions; but nonetheless gossip since it depends on individuals."

Gossip, we must admit, has a perennial interest for all of us. Personal chat is the current coin of conversational capital. Society lives by gossip as it lives by food. The most stupid rule in the world is to ignore personalities in discussion. To annihilate gossip would be to cut conversational topics in half. There is musical gossip, art gossip, theatrical gossip, literary gossip, and court gossip; there is political gossip, and fashionable gossip, and military gossip; there is mercantile gossip and commercial gossip of all kinds; there is physicians' gossip and professional gossip of every sort; there is scientists' gossip; and there is the gossip of the schools indulged in by masters and students all over the educational world.

Of all the gossip in the world the most prodigious and prolific is religious gossip.

Archbishops, bishops, deans, rectors, and curates are discussed unreservedly; and the questions put and answered are not whether they are apostolic teachers, but whether they are high, low, broad, or no church; whether they wear scarlet or black, intone or read, say "shibboleth" or "shibboleth."

The roots of gossip are deep in human interest; therefore, against the practically unanimous judgment of moralists, great reputations are more frequently produced out of chatter than destroyed by it. Discriminating individuals do not make enemies by personality, nor divide friends, since they talk with a heart full of love, with compassion for everyone, and with hatred against none. Gossip as a valid aspect of conversation is supported by one of the best of present-day academics; and I cannot do better than to cite, in concluding, what Mr. Mahaffy has said about it: "The subject which ought to be constantly intriguing is the examination of human character and human reasons. If the novel is such a popular type of literature, how can the novel in real life fail to attract an intellectual company? People of serious temper and philosophic habit will be able to confine themselves to large ethical views and the general dealings of men; but to average people, both men and women, and perhaps most of all to busy men who desire to find in society relaxation from their toil, that lighter and more personal kind of criticism on human affairs will prevail which is known as gossip.

It is futile to deny that there is no type of discourse more intriguing than this. But its immorality may easily become such as to shock honest minds, and the man who indulges in it too freely at the expense of others will probably have to pay the cost of it himself in the long run; for those who hear him will fear him, and will retire into themselves in his presence. On the other hand, nothing is more honorable than to stand forth as the defender or the palliator of the faults imputed to others, and nothing is easier than to expand such a defense into general considerations as to the purity of human motives, which will raise the conversation from its unwholesome grounds into the upper air."

CHAPTER IV

WHAT SHOULD GUESTS TALK ABOUT AT DINNER?

Guests' Talk During the Quarter of an Hour before Dinner—What Guests May Talk About—Talking to One's Dinner-Companion—Guests' Duty to Host and Hostess—The Dominant Note in Table-Talk—General and Tête-à-Tête *Conversation between Guests—*

The Raconteur at Dinner.

CHAPTER IV

WHAT SHOULD GUESTS TALK ABOUT AT DINNER?

"Good discourse is not to be obtained for the asking. Humor must first be granted in a sort of prelude for prolog; hour, company, and circumstances be suitable; and then at a proper juncture, the topic, the quarry of two hot minds, leap out like a deer out of the wood." Stevenson understood as well as Alice in Wonderland that something had to begin the dialogue. "You can't even drink a bottle of wine without opening it," asserted Alice; and every dinner guest, throughout the quarter of an hour before dinner, has sensed the sententiousness of her comment. Someone in writing about this critical period so conversationally difficult has contended that no person in his senses would think of wasting good talk in the drawing- room before dinner, but Professor Mahaffy thinks otherwise: "In the very forefront there stares us in the face that awkward period which even the gentle Menander notes as the worst possible for conversation, the short time during which people are assembling, and waiting for the announcement of dinner.

If the clever guy were not typically a greedy person, who would not display his gift without the benefit of complete and unhurried admiration, now is the true opportunity to demonstrate his talents. A brilliant thing said at the very start which sets people laughing, and makes them forget that they are waiting, may alter the whole complexion of the party, may make the silent and distant people feel themselves drawn into the sympathy of common merriment, and thaw the iciness which so often fetters Anglo-Saxon society. But since this capacity is not given to many, the typical man may content himself with having something ready to say, and this, if feasible, in response to the common query expressed or implied: Is there any news this afternoon?

There are few days that the daily paper will not afford to the intelligent critic something ridiculous either in style or matter which has escaped the ordinary public; some local event, nay, even some local tragedy, may suggest a topic not worth more than a few moments of attention, which will secure the interest of minds vacant, and perhaps more hungry to be fed than their bodies. Here therefore, if anyplace in the broad spectrum of discussion, the man or woman who wishes to be pleasant may risk to plan ahead, and bring with them something ready, only as the initial kick or starting point to make the evening flow well.

" However this may be, it is only with that communicative spirit which comes after eating and drinking that talkers warm up to discerning debate; thus in the drawing-room immediately before dinner, one can barely expect the conversation to center on anything except trifles.

At the time a guy extends his arm to the lady he is to take in to dinner, he must have something ready in the form of a comment, because if he walks in quietly, he is lost. There are a thousand and one nothings he may say at this moment. I know a brilliant guy who speaks eloquently for fifteen minutes about the old-fashioned habit of extending a lady the hand to lead her into supper, and whether or not that tradition was more kind and elegant than our current manner of approaching.

The topic is commonly posed, "What should guests speak about during a dinner?" I restrict my interrogation to guests, because there is a distinction between the directing of a dinner-conversation guest's and the guiding of the talk by host or hostess into necessary or interesting channels. Dinners, especially in diplomatic circles, are as often given to bring about dexterously certain ends in view as they are given for mere pleasure; and when this is the case it is necessary as well as gracious to steer conversation along the paths that it should go. A guest's first duty is to his dinner-companion, the person with whom, according to the prearranged plan of the hostess, he enters the dining-room and by whom he finds himself seated at table. His next obligation is to his hosts. He has also an abstract conversational responsibility to his next closest neighbor at dinner. It is every guest's obligation, too, to keep his ears open and be ready to engage in general chat should the host or hostess seek to attract all their visitors into any general debate.

The ideal response to the question, "What should guests at dinner speak about?" is, anything and everything, provided the discourse is tinctured with subtlety, discretion, and discernment. To one's dinner-companion, if he happens to be a close acquaintance, one might even forget to ban attire, sickness, and domestics. One can also, with caution, allow at free the traditionally banned discourse of "shop," on condition that such personal chat belongs to one's dinner-companion alone and is not pulled into the broader flights of the table-talk. While one chats to one's dinner-companion in a quiet voice, however, it demands great discernment not to appear to whisper under one's breath, or to say something to a left-hand neighbor which would not be proper for a right-hand neighbor to hear. When in general discourse, the practice some allegedly well-bred folks have of gazing furtively at any one visitor to inquire telepathically another's judgment of any comment is ill-tempered beyond the capacity of censure or the possibility of forgiveness.

At huge, formal meals, on the order of banquets, it would be difficult for all guests to include a host or hostess in their conversational groupings from each and every section of the table; only those guests placed near them may do this. But during small, informal meals all guests should, wherever possible, consider it their obligation to dedicate most of their talk to their host and hostess. I have witnessed guests at tiny meals of little more than six or eight covers go through the many courses of a three hours' eating, disregarding their host and hostess throughout the whole table-talk, while speaking volubly with others. There is something more owed to a host and hostess than just pleasantries on arrival and leave-takings on going. If the dinner-party is so enormous that all visitors cannot show them at the table the attention due them, the delinquent ones might at least seek an opportunity in the drawing-room, after guests have departed the dining-room, to pay their host and hostess the proper courtesy.

Hosts should never be made to feel that it is to their cook they owe their distinction, and to their table alone that guests pay visits.

To suggest that the prevailing note in table-talk should be light and amusing is going too far; yet discourse amongst dinner-companions should incline strongly to the humorous, to the light, to the slight change of views. There should be an adroit intermixing of light and serious conversation. I noticed once with considerable pleasure a smart blending of serious conversation with small chat at a dinner given to a prominent German scientist. A bright lady of my acquaintance found herself the one picked to entertain at dinner this foreigner and scholar. When she was presented in the drawing-room to the eminent man who was to take her in to dinner, her hostess opened the conversation by informing the noted guest that his new acquaintance, just that morning, had had conferred upon her the degree of doctor of philosophy, which was the reason she had been assigned as dinner-companion to so profound a man. The foreigner followed the conversational signal, relaying to his buddy his thoughts on the amount of American women pursuing higher education, et etc. Such a conversational situation was little conducive to small talk; but on the way from the drawing-room to the dining-table, this clever woman directed the talk into light vein by assuring the scholar and diplomat that there was nothing dangerous about her even if she did possess a university degree; that she would neither bite nor philosophize on all occasions; that she was quite as full of life and frolic as if she had never seen a university.

You can envision the influence of this vivacity upon the profoundest of men, and you can understand how this bright woman's aptitude at small chat made a friend of a prominent academician. As the evening went the discourse between these two veered from humor to solemn in a most delightful way. Apropos of a late book on some important topic not expurgated for newborns and sucklings, but written for thinking men and women, the German scientist requested if he may give his friend a copy, provided he agreed to glue carefully together the chapters inappropriate for frolicking feminine brains. Two days later she got the book with part of the margins pasted—which pages, of course, were the first ones she read.

When making an effort to dazzle in small chat, dinner-guests should remember that the line of demarcation between light banter and buffoonery may become dangerously fragile. One can talk lightly, but nicely; while buffoonery is just what the lexicographers define it to be: "Amusing people by clownish acts and by ordinary niceties." Gentle dullness ever loved a joke; and the fact that very often humorists, paid so highly in literature to perform, will not play a single conversational trick, is the best proof that they have the good sense to vote their hosts and companions capable of being entertained by something nobler than mere pleasantry. "When wit," says Sydney Smith, "is combined with sense and information; when it is in the hands of one who can use it and not abuse it (and one who can despise it); who can be witty and something more than witty; who loves decency and good nature ten thousand times better than wit,—wit is then a beautiful and delightful part of conversation." Opinions as to what good nature is would perhaps vary. "You may be good-natured, sir," observed Boswell to Doctor Johnson, "but you are not good-humored." The speech of men and women is diverse and variously characteristic. All people say "good morning," but no two of God's creatures say it alike. Their words range from a grunt to gushing exuberance; and one is as objectionable as the other. Even important matters may be spoken about in tones of badinage and good manners. Plato in his brilliant talks always gave his topic a border of exquisite wit, but underneath the delicate shell there was dependably a hard nut to be cracked. If good kindness above all is real, it will avoid becoming overflowing. The duplicity which says, "My lovely Mrs. So-and-so, I'm quite happy to see you; do sit right down on this bent pin!" is not good nature; it is sheer balderdash. Thoughtful dinner-guests take efforts not to dominate the discussion. They invite others of the group into their discourse, providing them chances of talking in their turn, and listening themselves as they do so: "You, Mr. Brown, will agree with me in this"; or, "Mr. Black, you have had more experience in similar circumstances than I have; what is your opinion?" The completeness of this talent of conversational charm lies in that rare gift, the ability of pulling people out, and is as useful and charming in visitors as in hosts.

The French have several dinner-table etiquette which to us appear weird. At any small lunch of eight or 10 people the discourse is always expected to be generic. The person who would try to begin a tête-à-tête conversation with the guest sitting next to him at the table would soon find out his mistake. General discussion is as much a part of the repast as the viands; and wo to the naive mortals who, seduced by small distances, start to converse among themselves. A diner-out must be able to hold his own in a discourse in which all types of distant, as well as close, participants take part. Of course, this requires tiny meals; but English-speaking individuals, even in small settings, do not seek general chat to such a degree. They consider it a challenging issue to execute the diagonal feat of addressing visitors from too great a distance. Dinner-companions, however, should be alert to others of the conversational group. A guest can as easily lead the talk into general paths as can a host or hostess. Indeed, it is gracious for him to do this, though it is not his duty. The duty lies entirely with a host or hostess. At any time through the dinner a guest can help to make conversation general: If someone has just told in a low voice, to a right-hand or left-hand neighbor alone, some clever impersonal thing, or a good anecdote, or some interesting happening suitable to general table-talk, the guest can get the attention of all present by addressing someone at the furthest point of the table from him: "Mr. Snow, Miss Frost has just told me something which will interest you, I know, and perhaps all of us: Miss Frost, please tell Mr. Snow about," et cetera. Miss Frost, therefore, speaking a bit louder so that Mr. Snow may hear, engages the attention of the whole table. The minute any one round the table calls the attention of the full dinner-group, dinner-companions should quickly quit their private discussions and engage in whatever general discourse may follow on the subject commonly brought. The thread of their tête-à-tête chat may be picked up later when the general table-talk is halted.

A narration or an anecdote should not be long drawn

out. A dinner-guest, or a host, or a hostess, is for the time being a conversationalist, not a lecturer. It is the unwritten rule of good dinner-talk that no one person round the table should retain the floor for more than a few brief lines. The point in tales should be brought out immediately, and no incident of great duration should be recalled.

A visitor in narrating any event might break his own narrative up into discussion by inviting into his chat, or recital, people who are interested in his pastime or in his experience.

Responses to

toasts at banquets may be slightly longer than the individual speeches of a single person in general table-talk; yet each dinner-speaker understands that even his answer runs the danger of being spoiled if prolonged beyond a few minutes.

There are never-failing topics of interest and untold material out of which to weave suitable dinner-talk, provided it is woven in the right way. And this weaving of talk is an art in which one may become proficient by giving it attention, just as one becomes the master of any other art by taking thought and probing into underlying principles. So in the art of talking well, even naturally fluent talkers need faithful pains to get beyond the point where they only happen to talk. They need to attain that conscious power over conversational situations which gives them precision and grace in adapting means to ends and a fine discrimination in choosing among their resources.

A one-sided conversation between companions is deadly unless discrimination is used in the matter of listening as well as talking. For instance:

Mr. Man: "Don't you find the notion of developing a huge riverfront road a beautiful one?"

Miss Brown: "Yes."

Mr. Man: "The New York drive is one of the joys of life; it gives more unalloyed pleasure than anything I know of."

Miss Brown: "Yes."

Unless under conditions suitable to listening and not to talking, Mr. Cook might feel like saying to Miss Brown, as a bright young man once said to a quiet, beautiful girl: "For heaven's sake, Miss Mary, say something, even if you have to take it back." While it is true that listening attentively is as valuable and necessary to thoroughly good conversation as is talking one's self, good listening demands the same discretion and discrimination that good talking requires. It is the business of any supposedly good conversationalist to discern when and why one must give one's companion over to soliloquy, and when and why one must not do so.

The dining-room is both an arena in which talkers fight with words upon a field of white damask, and a love-feast of discussion. If guests are neither hatefully disputatious, nor hypocritically humble, if they are generous, frank, natural, and wholly honest in word and mind, the impression they make cannot help being agreeable.

CHAPTER FIVE

TALK OF HOST AND HOSTESS AT DINNER

The Amalgam for Combining Guests—Hosts' Talk During the Quarter of an Hour before Dinner—Seating

Guests to Enhance Conversation—Number of Guests for the Best Conversation—Directing the Conversation at Dinner—Drawing Guests Out—Signaling for Conversation—General and Tête-à-tête *Conversation—Putting Strangers at Ease—Steering Talk Away from Offensive Topics—The Gracious Host and Hostess—An Ideal Dinner Party.*

CHAPTER FIVE

THE TALK OF HOST AND HOSTESS AT DINNER

A renowned practitioner of the social art by all accounts, Sydney Smith, once remarked of himself: "There is one gift I suppose I have to a surprising degree: there are compounds in nature called amalgams, whose characteristic it is to blend incongruous things.

I now possess an odd aptitude for blending various socially repulsive human elements because of my moral amalgamation.

His biographer continues, "And without a doubt, I have seen a party composed of elements as ill-sorted as could be imagined, dragged out and enticed together, till at last you would believe they had been born for each other." However, because this role of moral amalgamation requires such subtlety and delicacy, hostesses are justified in making use of whatever technical tools at their disposal. The first step in amalgamating a dinner party is to choose amiable people. Due to the random nature of dinner invitations, conversations are frequently a complete disaster. It is preferable to take the chance of offending than to put the conversation's flow in danger by inviting those who would disrupt it. It might be difficult to plan the inviting and seating of guests profitably when dinners are provided as part of commitments. However, the judgment that was just demonstrated may save or ruin a meal. Giving a series of meals and sending out the invites all at once is an excellent approach to get around the problem of hosts having duties to individuals with various preferences and interests. Mrs. X. is not upset if Mrs. Z. invites her to dinner the night after the dinner to which Mrs. Z. has invited Mrs. Y. The following step in the merger process should be to ensure that there is no lack of sensitivity while seating guests. A considerable deal of consideration should be given to the ingredients in this human salad in order to achieve the greatest outcomes. A brilliant guest should be seated where he can at least snatch crumbs of intellectual comfort if his near companions, though talkative, are not the best conversationalists; the talkative guest should be seated next to the usually taciturn, provided he is one who can be roused to conversation when thrown with talkative people. If not, one of the hosts should focus on encouraging conversation with the reticent but yet fascinating person. A shrewd hostess will think about seating visitors in relation to choosing and inviting them. Therefore, it is one of the auxiliary and wholly mechanical steps in the true art of amalgamation.

If hosts recall nothing that can attract a visitor to his comfort, they will remember most importantly the quarter-hour before dinner and start the actual conquest of amalgamation as their friends are gathering. They will bring forth their mines of things old and new and engage friendly guests in discussion by being animated and hospitable. The ore will be coined into different sums, big and tiny, as necessary.

In certain highly intellectual settings, men and women are expected to be well-educated and amusing enough that they don't need any literary or silly conversational aids. However, every host is aware of the technique of placing appropriate quotations, creative sayings, or smart limericks on place cards, as well as the encouragement they provide for conversation among dinner partners as the visitors are seated. However, the host and hostess' obligations do not cease when they provide their dinner guests a topic for conversation. This is the reason why, as Canon Ainger so eloquently put it, "a dinner party should be neither too big nor too tiny in order to be beneficial for anything, beyond the simple enjoyment of the cuisine. The second part of the epigram can be securely accepted; some long-forgotten genius stated that the number should never be fewer than that of the Graces or more than that of the Muses. Ten people at most, eight for perfection; otherwise, talk may either be conversational or it can grow and become broad, and the host or hostess just has to supervise as much as can be done so profitably.

The dinner gathering of 16–20 people is the danger that is the worst. Nowadays, having a good general discussion at a table with a few people is more of an exception than the rule due to our tendency of packing our rooms or tables and treating our social duties like debts from businesses. In fact, a lot of our young people haven't heard a group discourse in so long that they believe their sole responsibility in society is to speak to one person at a time. The effects of the trend of big dinner parties are really dangerous. No dinner table should be too big to prevent casual discussion in a truly decent society. General conversation is impossible, for instance, during a supper of thirty or forty people. At large banquets, general discussion is replaced by toasts and answers, but at small meals, it is polite for the host and hostess to take the initiative and steer the topic frequently along broad avenues. As I've already indicated, it's possible for visitors to be negligent as well as the host and hostess themselves when people ignore them during the many courses of a three-hour meal. A host and hostess should not ignore any one guest any more than any one guest should ignore them. If they sit at their own table, as I have occasionally witnessed hosts and hostesses do, acting in exactly the same way as if they were the most careless guest at another's table, they cannot reasonably expect their own guests to act anything other than petrified, no matter how naturally social they may be.

As a result, a host and hostess have a conversational obligation to the entire group of individuals gathered at their table and, in particular, to their right-hand neighbors, the guests of honor. A host and hostess' primary responsibility is to ensure that each visitor actively participates in the conversation at the table. introducing basic topics and inviting attendees to participate so they match each other. The foundation of all effective talking is this encouragement of common discourse. However, a lot of folks don't need to be dragged out. Above all, the special guest of the event, or the person who is best known for his or her humor or storytelling, should not be pressured or questioned at the onset, as if he were obviously being exploited by the corporation, advises Mr.

Mahaffy. Unless the guest is a stranger, it is safe to leave him alone.

As drawing out the people one finds themselves surrounded by in society will be covered in a future essay, I won't go into detail about it here other than to describe how a famous Charles Lamb pun gave a thoughtful host the ability to draw out a well-informed but reserved girl while also directing the conversation of the entire table to a topic of universal interest. Mr. White, we were speaking of punning as a form of wit, and it reminded me that I have heard Miss Black, at your left, repeat a clever pun of Charles Lamb—a retort he made when someone accused him of punning. This caught the attention of all his guests. He then turned the conversation with his close neighbor into a discussion of the advantages and disadvantages of punning. Can you offer us that pun, Miss Black? I'm sorry, I seem to have forgotten. Miss Black swiftly replied, "I'll try to remember that, yes: "'If I were punished," raising her voice a bit louder than while conversing with her close neighbors so that her host and everyone at the table could clearly hear her.

I shouldn't have a puny shed where I may rest my chastised head for every pun I've made.

As a result, Miss Black was not only brought into the conversation but also into it, where she became the focus of a lengthy broad debate on the highly impersonal yet fascinating topic of punning. The conversation soon turned back to private conversations amongst dinner guests as the discussion on puns veered off topic.

When the discussion has been tête-à-tête for too long, a host or hostess will instinctively know and will once more make it generic. When visitors pay close attention to their host and hostess, the conversation will inevitably spill over into other areas, especially if they are situated distant from the host and hostess. Even in casual conversation, a good narrative that is brief and concise is unquestionably a good thing. However, story-telling gets boring when the host or a visitor just "anecdotes" from the soup to the coffee. Anecdotes shouldn't be forced in; rather, they should emerge spontaneously as the discussion of several topics may do.

It is the host and hostess' responsibility to facilitate discussion for any strangers in a foreign place, and it is undoubtedly their joy to do so. It doesn't always follow that a host and hostess are familiar with every visitor. In certain cases, they have never even spoken to some of them. The formality of prior calls is discarded for various reasons, and an invitation is made to a friend's home visitor or a notable someone who is now nearby. Even if he isn't considered a guest of honor, the hostess should seat this visitor as close to herself as possible unless she feels completely comfortable giving that responsibility to someone else. In this way, she may get to know her new friend better and place the stranger on an equal footing with the other visitors who are well acquainted.

In their eagerness to please their guests, hosts and hostesses frequently notify guests that they are to dine with a very intellectual lady, and the woman is informed that she is to be the neighbor of a highly intelligent guy. On the other hand, it might be more tactful to say that although a certain person has the reputation of being exceptionally clever, he is, in truth, as natural as an old shoe and that all one needs to do to entertain him is to talk ordinarily about commonplace topics. This is because some people's powers are brought out by being put on their mettle. In 89 out of 100 instances, this is the case. The saying "A great man always lives a great way off" was coined by someone, and it is true that when we get to know truly great people, we discover that they are just as interested in everyday things as everyone else. In fact, the more intelligent a person is, the more they are interested in domestic matters. When Tennyson was a passenger aboard a steamboat traveling across the English Channel, several of the passengers seated across from him in the dining saloon discovered that their seatmate at the table was the famous poet. They listened intently, hoping for some pearl of wisdom to fall from the famous man's lips, when they heard the enthusiastic phrase, "What beautiful potatoes these are!" The host and hostess must use good judgment in this specific situation; they must know when it is safe to impress one visitor with the other's intelligence and when it would be fatal to do so. Imagine that as a result of each guest waiting for the other's brilliant flow of wit, there is profound quiet between two highly intriguing people whose intelligence the host and hostess had relied on to make their dinner a success, much to the dismay of the host and hostess!

Additionally, it is the responsibility of the host and hostess to subtly direct the conversation away from subjects that could offend a particular visitor. Every visitor they invite into their house deserves not only their attention but also their protection.

If a visitor is unable to conduct himself in a conversational manner due to some disability, the onus is on the hosts to step in and save the day. The host and hostess must exercise the utmost discretion and sensitivity while circling themes that are unpleasant to any visitor. This is because, in order to prevent one guest from being hurt or embarrassed, the offender himself must not be made to feel bad about his behavior. He can be completely unaware of the impact his remarks are having on those he doesn't know well, as he often is. any topic that is being Dangerously handled objects must be juggled out of sight, and the decision to juggle them must be kept a secret. Though it is perfectly acceptable to excuse oneself for changing the subject suddenly, there is nothing worse than telling someone else to "Change the subject" or "Let's change the subject." This is impolite and nasty behavior. Making talkers talk about something else unintentionally is known as conversation direction. Any guest may politely steer the conversation away from topics that are likely to offend sensitive or uneducated people, as well as the host or hostess. A group of philosophic minds were invited to a series of dinners, where the main topic of conversation was religious intolerance. Most people in the circle shared a liberal worldview and were well acquainted with one another. A visitor entered the group; only a select few knew that he was a devout Catholic. As the conversation veered toward religious topics, one of the guests intervened to reveal that the stranger was a Catholic by faith and upbringing. This was a really thoughtful and appropriate action to take. It informed the hostess of a reality she was unaware of and provided everyone present confidence in whatever they would say.

The discussion at their table will not be absorbed by a kind host and hostess. Instead of brazenly displaying their own brilliance, they will do the kind deed of providing a backdrop for others' cunning. In fact, either a man or a woman can thrive in this most polite of social skills without being clever or cerebral. The most brilliant individual in the world who selfishly monopolizes discourse at his own table will lose out to the host or hostess who exhibits subtlety and empathy when hosting a dinner party. If visitors are not able to leave a meal feeling better about themselves, the campaign of hospitality has failed. The pinnacle of hospitality is reached when the self-satisfaction on the hosts' and hostesses' faces exposes the delicate skill of convincing all of their visitors that they have made themselves fascinating. One day, one of the kindest but most dull of guys was joking about how he had been royally sidetracked at a dinner party.

He was at Mrs. X's, someone said.

How did you learn that?
"Indeed! Is there anything I don't know about her route? She could rival the nightingale by making a raven fly home.
The pinnacle of all social achievements is to be able to enhance the self-esteem of your visitors.
According to a well-known London hostess, "the perfect dinner party resembles nothing so much as a masterpiece of the jeweler's skill, in which the center is some crystalline gem in the shape of a brilliant and sympathetic hostess, around whom the guests are grouped in an

efficient setting." The need for a host to demonstrate a crystalline gem in this work of jewelry artistry would seem to be equally important. Care in making the conversation engaging is just as important as care in preparing the food if you want your dinner party to be a success. Successful hosts and hostesses take just as much care to avoid conversational deaths as they do to avoid offensive food. While painstakingly cleaning the crystal and planning the meal that will make their table a joy, they keep in mind that their visitors' intellects must be as well-satisfied as their eyes and stomachs.

CHAPTER SIX

INTERRUPTION IN CONVERSATION

More than anything else, interruptions end conversations. The verbose talker, who despite his verbal prowess is by no means a conversationalist, refuses to acknowledge that discussion includes a partnership and that each participant in this group of people with shared interests has a right to take turns participating in the conversation. He doesn't pay attention to the other people in the conversation and enters early on in their sentences with his own speaking. He keeps talking notwithstanding the contempt he causes in the minds of every well-educated, discriminating conversationalist who hears him since interrupting has become such a habit for him. Even the finest talkers occasionally interrupt during a discussion, but the unconscious, harsh interruption of a chronic interrupter and the inadvertent, deliberate disruption of a cultured talker are both extremely obvious and differ

greatly from one another.
We have become accustomed to believing that children are the only ones who interrupt, yet, in the style of the French salon, it is actually adults who do the offenses! The unfortunate thing about this constructive phase of interruption is that frequent interrupters seldom even realize how often they actually knock their converses' words back into their mouths by breaking into their remarks. James Walter Ferrier received the following tribute from Robert Louis Stevenson: "He

was the only man I ever knew who did not habitually interrupt." Now, those of you reading this may not think that you violate the first rule of polite conversation—"Thou shalt not interrupt"—but consider the slim chance you have to get away with it when only one of Stevenson's friends was exonerated in this case. Before one can stop interrupting, he or she must become aware that they are doing so. Because conscious interruption stops being interruption, it is the unconsciousness that makes the crime. When a competent talker becomes aware that he has interrupted his converser's speech, he avoids interruption by waiting to hear what was about to be stated. I beg your pardon, which is the polite way of stating "Pardon me for seeming hesitant to listen to you; I actually am both willing and delighted to hear what you have to say," used to break off his own speech right away. He also shows that he is willing by waiting for the other person to finish the thinking he started. What better evidence is there that listening is a necessary part of conversation?

One stage of conversation interruption is due to a simple, anxious inability to listen. The interruption of the roving gaze is what indicates that one's words have not been understood. The person next to you must be bored since my chat is only reaching one of your ears and not the other, the talker muttered somewhat testily to the diner whose oblivious and late responses had been breaking the thought's flow until it became intolerable. She was probably only slightly less annoying than the man, whose propensity of inattention caused him to become so oblivious that, on one occasion, his conversation partner had just ended when he began abstractly: "Yes, very unusual, very odd," and repeated the same narrative.

Another stage of interrupting develops from the jerky talker who, instead of responding to his conversation partner's statements with questions and answers, affirmations, and rejoinders, but instead waits anxiously for a moment to chime in with his own ideas. The author Dean Swift described this type of talker as follows: "There are people whose manners will not permit them to directly interrupt you, but what is almost as bad, will discover abundance of impatience, and lie upon the watch until you have done, because they have started something in their own thoughts, which they long to be delivered of. As a result, they limit their creativity, which could otherwise cover over a hundred equally brilliant things and be presented much more organically.

In the meantime, they are so removed from what is happening that their minds are entirely focused on what they have in reserve. A story or comment will endure. We are not required to resent every second that cuts into our allotted time, to interrupt our companion with our looks, or to consider him an obstruction to our much better remarks.

A less offensive form of interrupting is when a conversationalist is so eager to demonstrate his quick perception that he assumes to know what you are going to say before you have finished your sentence in your own mind and to put an interpretation on your arguments before you are done stating them. This form of interrupting often results from kind thought rather than from arrogance. His interpretation is frequently exactly the opposite of yours while also being identical, and whether the explanation is correct or incorrect, it only serves to break up the line of thought. Against this type of interruption, a writer waxed irate in the New England Magazine as early as 1832: "I have heard individuals praised for this, as indicating a rapidity of mind that arrived at the end before the other was halfway through. But if someone stole my words from my mouth or my money from my pocket, I would feel just as inclined to attack that person. Such a habit may be a testament to one's abilities, but not necessarily to their modesty or good nature. What else could it be but a statement along the lines of, "My dear sir, you are making a very bungling piece of work with that sentence of yours; allow me to finish it for you in proper style. Although one may feel that the author should have saved his verbal chastisement for more grating instances of impertinent interruption, it is still true that those who allow their conversation partners to finish their sentences without worrying about being interrupted are more considerate. Talkers who are glib assume that those who express themselves more deliberately are somehow inferior. conversation is less interesting. The pig is one of the most rapidly loquacious of animals, yet no one would say that the pig is an attractive conversationalist. Pope may have taken his time creating the mosaic of symbols that so beautifully expresses the idea that "Words are like leaves, and where they most abound, they flourish," It is unusual to find much fruit of reason beneath, yet his deliberateness did not lessen the lines' insight, fascination, or beauty. If given the freedom to communicate in their own unique style, slow talkers only serve to enhance the allure of any group. Why should we appreciate characters in books and plays more than in real life? The best kind of talk is where each speaker is most fully and candidly himself, where, if you should shift the speeches around from one to another, there would be the greatest loss in significance and perspicuity, according to Stevenson. It is dramatic like an impromptu piece of acting where each should represent himself to the greatest advantage.

Another way that excellent discourse is interrupted is by the Gradgrinds of society, who are always descending upon us with some unpleasant and needless information. They tell you that the tragedy happened on Tremont Street, not Boylston, and they raise an important point in the air to show that it was Mr. Jones' elder sister, not his youngest, who was traveling when the San Francisco earthquake occurred. They feel it necessary to interrupt the speaker if someone claims that an incident happened on the tenth of the month because they just so happen to know that it actually happened on the ninth. People frequently act as their own Gradgrinds, stopping mid-narration to fix some insignificant error that has no bearing whatsoever on what they are saying.

Many otherwise competent speakers occasionally suffer from aphasia, which causes them to forget the most basic and well-known word at precisely the wrong time—the word that is essential to the point they want to make. Elderly folks experience this more frequently, and it was on one such instance that I saw a reasonably youthful catchphrase addict use her favorite term as a red lamp to interrupt better, though more halting, speech. The dignified matron pleaded, "Mr. Black was telling me today about Mr. White's appointment to what do you call that office? The glib undergraduate, who had been using these words to describe everyone and everything, impertinently suggested, "Just call it anything, Mrs. Gray, a bandersnatch, or a buttonhook, or a battering-ram." She continued to do so until she found a new catchphrase to serve as the main topic of her conversation. Particularly from youth, the frailties and mellowed wisdom of age deserve the utmost respect; in this case, deference in helping the elderly woman find her words would have been more elegant than pleasant, even if the latter were of a less petty sort.

Both interruptions from outside the conversational group and interruptions that occur directly during the conversation suffer. Charles Lamb suggested the wellbeing of Herod, King of the Jews, after bringing extremely young children into adult society! Society is not a place for young children, and if older children are allowed to attend, they should be taught to pay close attention and participate modestly in conversations. A child should be included in the conversation if he offers an opinion or a question about the subject being discussed. In this situation, his opinions should be taken into account on par with the more experienced opinions of his elders, regardless of how immature they may be; he should be given full membership in the conversational group. He should be completely sent away, or this.

In an issue of this nature, there are no half measures. Both the child's chatter and the parent's repeated requests to "remain quiet" or "to be seen and not heard" are disruptive. Furthermore, many children's inherent ability to communicate clearly has been crushed by adults who stifle whatever words they try to say. From the time she was seven years old until she was fifteen, the parents of a bright young lady I know put so much pressure on her that she developed the early habit of never opening her lips without first receiving the mother's or father's approval. When a youngster is treated in this way as a young child, his uniqueness and spontaneity are stifled, and he grows up to be shy and hesitant in speaking. Send the kids out to themselves where they may at least communicate their opinions to someone their own age, or let them talk while simultaneously teaching them how to converse. The finest conversational lesson a youngster can learn is to learn not to interrupt and to realize that he must either speak in accordance with the mannerisms of truly polite discourse or be sent away.

It's frequently said that kids don't belong at the dinner table, where even passable conversation is expected. This point of view is undoubtedly valid when it comes to formal dinners, but the family dinner table is the ideal setting for teaching kids the virtues of polite conversation and engaging table topics. To this aim, when the family sits down to eat, disagreements and hostilities should be put aside. As much as possible, parents should ensure that their children talk about only amusing and intriguing events at the dinner table. First of all, Mr. Mahaffy continues, "let me advise individuals who feel that it is not worth the bother to converse in their family circle, or who read the newspaper at meals, that they are making a mistake that has far-reaching effects. It is almost as awful as those convent schools or women academies where mealtimes are either silent or in a foreign language. There is no denying that practice is required for dialogue, regardless of what one may believe of the worth of theory. This practice must be sought out among individuals who are close and unafraid to voice their opinions at home. The only way young people may enter the world with the one and only universal introduction to society agreable speech and manners is in this way and only this way.." The Outlook just made some excellent comments about infringing on young people's social and conversational rights, therefore I've transferred a portion of the piece to these pages. The editorial underlined the educational benefits of engaging in polite conversation at home: "The conversation at the dinner table is the most significant educational opportunity in the house.

Children who grew up in families where the conversation covered all major life interests and ran on broad lines would agree that nothing provided them with a more authentic education or gave them a better sense of joy. This may be one reason why some American

If children are in the right environment, they will not be intrusive or impertinent; make room for their interests, their questions, and the problems of their experience; for there are young as well as old perplexities; encourage them to talk, and meet them more than halfway by the utmost hospitality to the subjects that interest and puzzle them; give them serious conversations; and give them respect. The child is always looking ahead, peering curiously into the mysterious world around him, hearing strange voices from it, getting wonderful glimpses into it. Some people make the mistake of "talking down" to their children; of turning the conversation at the table into a kind of elaborate "baby-talk," not realizing that they are depriving their children of hearing older people talk about the world in which they live.

Sits at the table and listens; it is a human spirit, eager, curious, wondering, surrounded by mysteries, silently taking in what it does not understand today, but which will take possession of it next year and become a torch to light it on its way.

It is through association with older people that these fructifying ideas come to the child; it is through such talk that he finds the world he is to possess. The talk of the family ought not, therefore, to be directed at him. But it must always remember him and create room for him."

This story about a young son of one of Chicago's clever men is relevant to how much kids enjoy good conversation. Guests were present, and the boy was sitting quietly and listening to his elders converse intelligently when his father suggested to Paul that it was late and perhaps he should go to bed. Another and as profound a childish appreciation comes from the historic city of our American Cambridge: "Please, father, let me remain; I do appreciate engaging talk." One of its representative families' little daughters had spent hours upstairs, trying to hear the dialogue downstairs. Unconsciously aware of his just right to occasionally converse with older people, the young son of a prominent Atlanta family was expressed naively when visiting friends on a plantation, "Mother dear, while I've been lying here all alone you were having such a liberal time downstairs," when her mother entered the little one's room after her guests had left. When asked by his host why he liked being in the country, John said, "I enjoy it here because you let me chat every day at the table." John's response to the question, "Don't they let you speak every day at home, John?" was a rare praise to his older pals and their interest in child-life. "Oh, when father says 'give the youngster a chance,' then they let me talk."

Poor table service is another external and discouraging conversational disruption. There can be no meaningful discourse at a table when the dialogue is often cut off by verbose orders to the staff. A hostess who takes delight in the discourse her guests have at the table makes sure the maid or butler serving it is adequately trained beforehand so that any queries from guests won't disrupt the conversation. If the serving maid or butler has to speak with the host or hostess for whatever reason, it should be done quietly so as not to disrupt the discussion. However subtly the servant accomplishes this, the discussion is cut short by the sheer fact that the host or hostess's focus is distracted from the topic at hand for even a little period of time. Effective assistance translates to effective management both at home and in the workplace. A hostess should take offense if her table is served improperly 350 days out of the year, since this prevents conversation at the table. She would have a skilled butler or maid if she were competent herself. She would be able to tell whether a maid or butler could be taught effectively by dismissing them and replacing them with someone who could. The "Russian" form of dining-table serving is preferred over all others so that conversations won't be interrupted, and it's becoming as common in America as it is abroad .

[A] A host and hostess may unintentionally interrupt conversation at the table due to the environment they foster. There is nothing more distasteful to guests than to observe that their host is anxious lest the arrangements of the hostess miscarry, that their hostess is making herself quite wretched by a fear that the dishes will not be prepared to perfection, or that their hostess is fretting over the fact that the food will not be prepared to perfection, or over the fact that the guests will not behave themselves properly. Recently, I saw the hostess at a dinner get so upset about an accident that destroyed a priceless salad dish that she began to cry. As a consequence, it required a lot of work from a kind and selfless visitor to maintain the conversation's pleasant flow. How much more deft and lovely was the way another hostess handled the same circumstance. The butler's pantry was where the visitors were startled by a crash, and everyone could tell by the tinkling sound that it was cut glass. This was not only a charming, informal way of smoothing out an awkward situation, but it gave the poor butler the necessary confidence to finish serving the dinner after a few quiet words of instruction were given by the hostess, "I hope there is enough glass in reserve so that none of you dear people will have to drink champagne from teacups." If the hostess had been disturbed about the situation, the staff would have heard her irritation, which may have led to more than one accident.

A hostess ought to In dinner-giving, as in life, it is the job of brilliance to convert misfortune into benefit. yet "be mistress of herself tho China fall."

An accomplished diner-out recalled being at a dinner party where, "from the time a portion of the ceiling collapsed, the guests were as joyful as crickets," obviously undertakers paid to lament for the joints and birds in the dishes.

One of the most irritating barriers to ripple discourse is interruptions from inside the conversational group, and interrupts from outside are equally awful. What enjoyment can be found in a two-person, three-person, or four-person discussion if every other comment interrupts the mental process? Frequent allusions to topics completely unrelated to the issue at hand give dialogue a jerky, sputtering ineffectiveness similar to how briefly inserting a spigot in a faucet hampers an equal flow of water from a tank. People who have a genuine appreciation for excellent conversation do not let unnecessary interruptions ruin the flow and enjoyment of their interactions with friends and acquaintances. And those who do allow these interruptions are only drivels, not conversationalists.

CHAPTER SEVEN

POWER OF FITNESS, TACT AND USING NICETY IN BUSINESS WORDS

The Secret to Being Able to Use Tactful and Vivid Words in Business—Essential Training Required for the Nice Use of Words—Why Fostering the Social Instinct Strengthens Business Persuasion—Why Business Success Depends Upon Nicety and Tact More Than on Any Quality of Force—

CHAPTER SEVEN

POWER OF FITNESS, TACT AND USING NICETY IN BUSINESS WORDS

A component of business language has to do with social grace. The phrase "the social touch of commercial language" first seems out of place. The majority of business is force, to be true, but where force would fail, a charming demeanor often succeeds. A man's business interests are more dependent on social instinct and manners training than would first seem. For illustration:

Customer: "I need a tin of black "Cobra" boot polish," as they enter the shop.

Do you want polish for the kind of shoes you are wearing? The dealer apologized, "Sorry, lady, we do not have 'Cobra,' since we are rarely requested for it."

If you inform a client suddenly, "We do not have such-and-such a brand in stock," the result is that she will turn and go. This is not businesslike since it is not courteous, pleasant, or diplomatic. A customer's judgment is also instantly questioned when she is informed that the brand she specifies is not often requested. By failing to assume, the minute he mentioned her shoes, that she wore high-quality clothing, had excellent taste, or had common sense, or anything of the such, the dealer in this scenario missed an opportunity to get the customer's attention. He might have greatly enhanced his response by using his social instinct. Giving her a non-committal, diplomatic remark will immediately establish good connections and provide you the opportunity to steer the conversation to another topic with ease and elegance.

Dealer: "Do you like 'Cobra' polish, madam? We find this brand more generally dependable and preferred for high-grade shoes such as you wear."

Speaking with a telling expression relies as much on how one says something as it does on what one really says, whether in a corporate setting or a social one.

What is the key to being able to craft clever and compelling sentences? A secret perhaps? Some people always use the proper words in the appropriate context. How did they discover that they could do this? How did they learn? How did they develop the talent of expression into fine art? Or were they born with this talent? Or, if there is a secret to expertise, do skilled wordsmiths jealousy preserve it? In that case, why?

Artists who play the piano, play the violin, paint, draw, or sing are all proud of the tenacious practice that leads to their accomplishment. Why shouldn't ready authors and ready speakers have the same pride in their honest work? Are they so proud of their "natural aptitude for expression" that they hardly recognize the steps they have taken to get where they are by stumbling but persevering? A few great souls and wordsmiths have been extremely open about how they developed their skill at phrase construction. Robert Louis Stevenson, who was equally adept at speaking and writing, once said of himself: "Though regarded as a slacker at school, I was always busy on my own private ends, which was to learn to use words. I kept two books in my pocket, one to read and one to write in. As I walked, my mind was busy fitting what I saw with appropriate words.

As I sat by the roadside, a penny version book would be in my hand, to note down the features of What therefore is the fundamental instruction required for the polite use of language? It is a widely held belief that having a large vocabulary alone causes ideas to effortlessly flow from one's mouth or writing. But is this really the case? To be sure, one should have a mastery of language; one should be familiar with more adjectives than the general expressions "terrible, ferocious, fine, lovely," which are often used carelessly by those who are unconcerned with particular adverbs. However, using a vocabulary well is just as important as having one. In fact, every talker or writer's success is doomed to failure if they can't accurately represent their ideas on an effective backdrop using their terminology alone. It is worse to use a large vocabulary carelessly than to possess none.

When poet Keats penned those famous words, "A beautiful thing brings delight for all time.

It becomes more lovely,"

the first line was as follows:

"A beautiful object brings on continual delight.

The line, "A thing of beauty is a constant joy," persisted despite the author's numerous attempts to improve it for many months until the straightforward word "forever" finally came to him, "A thing of beauty is a joy forever." Then he had it, and he knew he had it—the essential note, the exact word. Certainly, the word "forever" was a part of Keats's vocabulary. When the editor of a magazine asked one of the most revered piano virtuosi in the world to provide biographical information and photographs for an article on musical composers, the pianiste had not yet published any compositions, and the gracious response swung readily into line: "If your article is to deal exclusively with musical composers, I cannot be included. The pianiste could have said, "of which I am proud," but a modest phrase must express honest pride—"my reputation as a pianiste which I guard sedulously," or "defend zealously." No, this the exactness and simplicity of true art rejected. Then came the simple, perceptive phrase, "my reputation as a pianiste which I guard sedulously," or "defend zealously."

What good are all the exquisitely colored tapestry strands in the world, stretched out before a tapestry weaver, if he cannot create flawless patterns with them by using his colors sparingly here and lavishly there?

More than any other quality of force, business success depends on the same nicety in the use of words that chooses the tactful expression, the modest and simple phrase, in the drawing-room; the sort of nicety that is unobtrusive exactness and delicacy; an artistry that in no way labels itself skilful. But underneath it all, the woof of the process is social skiing.

Conversation is reciprocal, good conversationalists can't talk to their best advantage without allies, as in whist, it takes a group to accomplish what a single genius at the instrument can't, good conversation doesn't distinguish between subjects; it denotes a difference in talkability, the different levels of talkability, how easily one can improve one's conversational skills, etc.

Good conversation, then, is like a well-played game of whist: each player must give and take; deal regularly to all the players; signal and respond to signals; follow suit or to trump with pleasantry or jest. And neither you nor any other player can win the game if even one refuses to be guided by its rules. It is the combination which affects what a single whist-playing genius could not. Because it is like a break.

Which guys perform best with the greatest players when held up at tennis? Satisfactory conversation does not depend on whether it is between those intellectually superior or inferior, between strangers or acquaintances, or whether each party to the conversation talks with due recognition of its first principles, said Sir Foppling Flutter; and few would refuse to admit that fortunate circumstances of companionship are as much a factor of good conversation as is native cleverness. A good converser knows exactly how the ball should return to him and feels betrayed if his partner is not even looking to catch it, much less showing any intention of tossing it back on precisely the right curve. "The habit of interruption," according to Bagehot, "is a symptom of mental deficiency; it proceeds from not knowing what is going on in other people's minds."

Henry Thomas Buckle claims that given discussion, which is characterized by adherence to all of its unwritten laws, "Men and women then range themselves into three classes or orders of intellect." The highest class can be distinguished by their preference for the discussion of ideas. Discussion is the most enjoyable of all conversations, if the company is up to it. It is the highest type of talk, but suited only to the highest type of individuals. Therefore, a person who in one circle might observe a prudent silence may in another veer off into veering off into veering off. Because of the Protean characteristic of man, the majority of us can converse to some extent with everyone; nevertheless, the genuine conversation that awakens the best in us only occurs with our unique spiritual brothers, which is why I believe that excellent conversation most often occurs among friends. In fact, both the setting and the talk as well as the tool of friendship. The finest social interaction is thus only possible when there is equality, as

Hazlitt noted in one of his charming essays: "In general, wit shines only through reflection. You must follow your company's lead; you must ascend when they ascend and descend when they descend. You must take care to prevent your good deeds and wise references from being thrown away like the proverbial pearls. What a test it is to ask a stupid question and discover that the fundamentals are not comprehended! You are quickly knocked to the ground; others who don't know the figure cease talking like a country dance. However, it is worthwhile to listen to an adept or illuminati group speak while they are discussing an issue.

At its best, conversation is one of the most pleasant intellectual stimulants; at its worst, it is one of the most intellectually deadening. Better to remain as quiet as a deaf-mute than to indulge recklessly in barbaric social interaction, if we are to have a growing generation of fine talkers.

One can easily imagine a sage like Emerson the victim of

conceited prigs, listening to their vapid conversational performances, and can readily understand why he considered conversation between two congenial souls the highest form of communication; however, really clever people dislike to compete in a race with talkers who rarely speak from the abundance of their hearts and often from the emptiness of their heads.

According to Mr. Mahaffy, "to assert that they depend wholly upon natural abilities is one of the commonest and most widely-repeated popular misconceptions.

Marked conversational skills are to some degree innate and in some ways learned.

founded on the fallacy that nature and art are incompatible, that nature only refers to the spontaneous and unplanned, and that art only refers to the obviously researched and manufactured.

Ask any youngster of five or six years old, wherever in Europe, to draw.

You can always get about the same results by giving a man's figure.

Therefore, you might argue that this is how a youngster would naturally depict a guy, notwithstanding how artificial it is. You would either ascribe this to a rare talent or exceptional training if one or two out of a thousand kids made a decent effort. Why? There need not be artificiality or affectation in talk that is consciously cultivated; no more indeed than it is affectation to eat with a fork because one knows that it is preferable to eat with a spoon.

Canon Ainger has positively said that "Conversation may be improved if only people would take pains and have a few lessons. Therefore, it appears that the best way to understand conversation is to be aware of the flaws and mistakes that it is susceptible to, and from there, for each person to formulate personal maxims for the regulation of conversation, as it only requires a few talents that the majority of men are not born with, or at the very least may not acquire, without any great genius or study. Because everyone has the ability to be agreeable, even if they don't shine in company, and because there are hundreds of people who are qualified for both roles but are only tolerated due to a very small number of flaws, Lord Lennox writes about Lady Blessington in his Drafts on My Memory, "In youth she did not give any promise of the charms for which she was afterwards so conspicuous, and which, in the first half of the nineteenth century, in the first half of the nin

Plato said: "Whosoever seeketh must know that which he seeketh for in a general notion, for otherwise how shall he know it when he hath found it? The average person, when he probes even slightly into the art, is as surprised as was Molière's bourgeois gentilhomme upon discovering that he had spoken prose for forty years.

When all people cultivate the art of conversation as assiduously as the notably good talkers of the world have done, there will be a general feast of reason and flow of soul; each will then say to the other, in Milton's words, "Each will say to the other, in the language of his own heart, that which he seeks in good conversation, even in abstract fashion.

"I lose track of time talking to thee."

www.ingramcontent.com/pod-product-compliance
Lightning Source LLC
LaVergne TN
LVHW010545160826
845677LV00013B/3006

9798353252580